All Color Book of
Oriental Carpets and Rugs

Stanley Reed

CHARTWELL
BOOKS, INC.

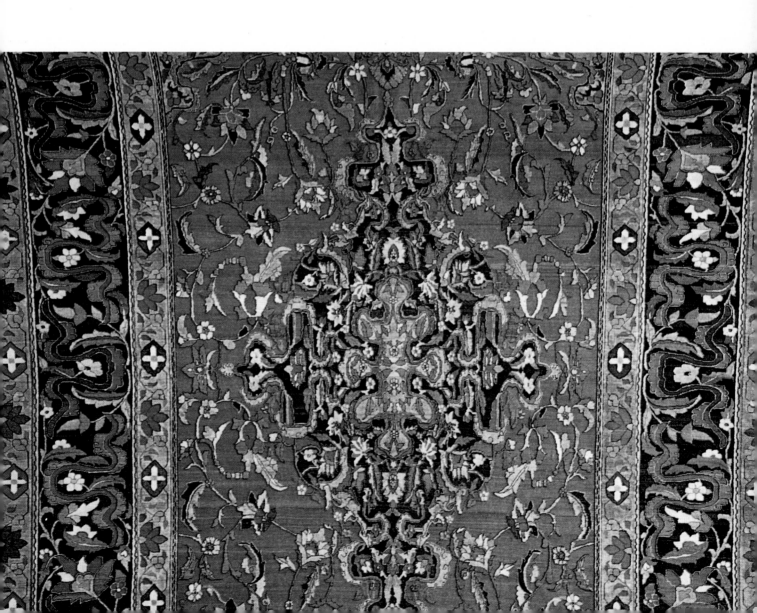

Contents

This edition published in 1990 by
The Hamlyn Publishing Group,
a division of The Octopus Publishing Group Limited,
Michelin House
81 Fulham Road
London SW3 6RB
for
CHARTWELL BOOK, INC
A Division of BOOKSALES, INC.
110 Enterprise Avenue
Secaucus, New Jersey 07094

© 1972 Octopus Books Limited

ISBN: 1-55521-619-6

Produced by Mandarin Offset
Printed and bound in Singapore

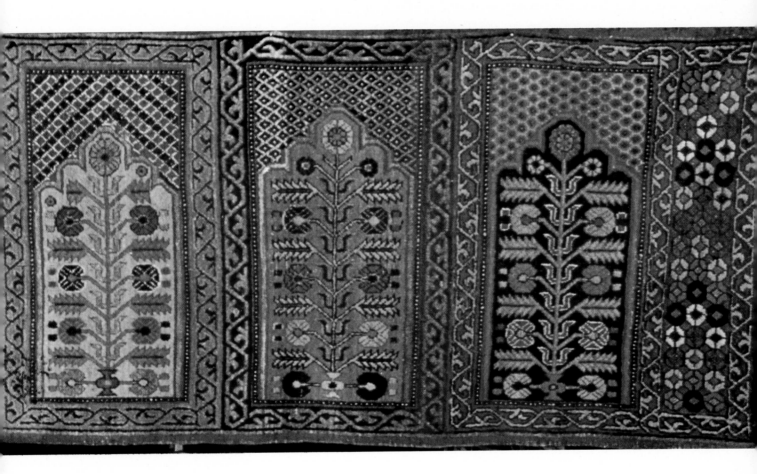

Introduction

This is a subject which knows no beginning and no end. No beginning, because until a few years ago no proof whatever existed that what we know as Oriental rugs and carpets could have been produced prior to the Christian era, and no end, because such products are still being made today in the same way as in those far off days. Before delving into the historical and technical details of this fascinating subject, it is necessary to define exactly what is meant by an Oriental rug, or carpet. It is true that machine-made carpets and rugs are now manufactured in some parts of the East, particularly Japan, but the definition we are seeking is of a hand-made, knotted product, made in any of the traditional areas between Turkey and China. Some licence must be given, however, to include certain aspects of Balkan production, the early carpets of Egypt, and passing mention of Spain. Also included are the pileless fabrics used as hangings, divan covers or floor coverings, and known by various names, but most popularly as Kelims.

It is also necessary to define what is meant by 'rug' and 'carpet'. Throughout this book the English version of these terms will be used. That is, a rug is any piece smaller than 9ft. × 6ft. From this size upwards the term 'carpet' will be used. There are two exceptions to this rule. A long and narrow piece is a runner, and a carpet of size 12ft. × 6ft. or larger, but in that proportion, is a Kelleye. The reason for this explanation is that in America the term 'scatter rug' is used for small pieces, 'rug' is used for large ones, and carpets refer to machine-made fitted carpeting with which we are not concerned.

The Historical Background

In view of the comparatively recent discovery of a rug dating from the fifth century BC (now known as the Pazyryk rug), in the wild and mountainous region of Gorny-Altai, it is now believed that the first hand-knotted carpets ever to be woven were made in Persia. Time alone will tell if this is true or not, when some future expedition uncovers more of the treasures of the Old World.

From this time onwards we are left with no actual examples, apart from some fourth century textiles from Egypt, which, although with a form of pile, are not to be classed with the true product, until the thirteenth century–these latter pieces being of Turkish origin. They were taken from the Mosque of Ala-ad-Din in Konia, and are now in the Museum of Islamic Art, in Istanbul. Even here the dating is doubtful.

This is the real beginning of the unbroken history of the craft, for although the next two or three centuries leave us little in the way of rugs themselves, and many of these not fully authenticated, it was an era of pictorial evidence, and countless paintings abound, particularly by Italian and Dutch masters, showing rugs and carpets as decoration either on the floor or thrown over tables. Some rugs have even acquired an artist's name, and one can read of 'Holbein' and 'Lotto' rugs, signifying the design painted by these artists.

Between the time of the Pazyryk and Konia examples stories come down to us of fabulous carpets, particularly through the writings of Marco Polo who, speaking of Asia Minor said, 'The best and handsomest carpets in the World are wrought here, and also silks of crimson and other rich colours'.

Another story concerns the fabulous 'Spring of Chosroes' carpet, from Ctesiphon. This was obviously not a knotted pile carpet as we know it. The size was reputed to be sixty cubits square – a cubit being the length of the forearm from elbow to the end of the middle finger, approximately 1ft. 6in. This would make the carpet about 90ft. × 90ft., a formidable size in any material. Apparently it was woven of silk, the pattern being representative of a garden, with streams, pathways, lawns and trees, the branches and flowers of which were made of precious stones of various colours. The object of the carpet was to create an illusion of spring time during the winter months for King Chosroes. Alas, the Persian Empire fell to the Arab invaders in 637 AD and the famous carpet was carried away to be cut up and divided amongst the conquerors as booty. It is said that several pieces found their way into the Baghdad bazaar. This carpet must have been of tapestry or flat weave type from its description. It is inconceivable to think of a piece of this size, with knotted pile, and bejewelled as well.

Early in the sixteenth century the position became much clearer. Turkey and Persia were producing great quantities of carpets, and some of these were being sent to all parts of the known world – to Egypt, North Africa, Spain, Venice of course, and through this great city to the Continent of Europe and England. Eastwards, the craft spread into India, and to Turkestan and China, although the latter may already have developed the art independently. This state of affairs lasted until the latter part of the seventeenth century, when a general decline set in, and it was not until the middle of the nineteenth century that the art was revived, this time due not to court patronage, but to commercial considerations. Today, once again, production, quality-wise, is at a low ebb, and this time it is possible that the end of the road is in sight. Eventually the hand-knotted product must cease to exist, apart from a few prestige pieces.

Unlike the sculptor or painter who is able to carry his own idea through from conception to finality, the 'carpet maker' is a complex body of people who perform various tasks, some very menial and none completely satisfactory in themselves, and it only needs a breakdown in one function for the whole operation to collapse.

Some Technical Details

The definition of an Oriental carpet or rug is a 'hand knotted product'. Before the hand knotting, however, many processes have to be performed. Wool mainly, and silk rarely, are the chief materials for the pile, whilst either cotton or wool will be needed for the foundation. These raw materials must be sorted, scoured and spun into yarn before the important dyeing procedure. Today, of course, these materials can be purchased already spun, and even dyed to specification, and most of the city-made, and commercially contracted carpets now being produced are made from machine spun yarns. Before this was possible, however, and indeed, in some of the more inaccessible places today, the sheep are locally bred, and every process of manufacture has to be carried out on the spot. All these preparatory processes require great skill, but the weavers are the people who actually produce the end product. However, these weavers are not creative artists in themselves. In the cities and manufacturing centres, even back to the days of court manufacture, they must be guided by designs conceived by artists of the first order and painstakingly drawn upon squared paper—one square for each knot of the carpet. In rural areas and amongst the nomadic peoples other methods of acquainting the weavers with the design formulae are used, such as drawing in the sand, or having the sequence of colours read or sung out to them. With repetition and long experience, especially in the making of pieces with tribal or other distinctive patterns, the weaver can memorize the sequences and at this stage he or she can work alone without the aids mentioned above.

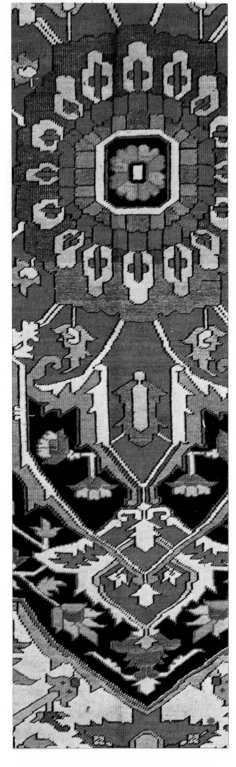

After the weaving, the carpet has to be sheared and washed, usually in local water or at some central point where the properties of the water are known and recommended. The chemical washing process to which certain modern pieces are subjected is done in Western countries to suit the particular taste of the market.

Basically there are two types of knot used throughout the Orient. The Ghiordes or Turkish knot (which is a full knot) and the Senneh or Persian knot (which is a half knot and can be left-handed or right-handed). Strangely enough, although the Pazyryk rug is attributed to Persia it is made with the Ghiordes knot. Another strange fact is that the Senneh rugs of Persia are usually, although not always, made with the Ghiordes knot. It is not known how these names came to be used, and perhaps it would be better if they were called just Turkish and Persian, or full and half knots, leaving the town names out of it altogether.

The dyeing process still involves locally made dyestuffs (of animal and vegetable origin) in some instances, particularly in country districts, but of course, modern synthetic dyes form the major proportion of those used today.

Until the middle of the nineteenth century all dyes were of natural origin, and the secrets of the craft were well guarded by the dye masters. These skills tended to run in families, and the recipes were handed down from father to son. Even after the invention of artificial dyes there was resistance to their use, particularly in Persia, where they were banned until the turn of the century.

Persia

The art of the Oriental carpet never reached greater heights than those achieved in Persia (or Iran as it is now called) during the Sefavi dynasty of the sixteenth and seventeenth centuries. The rulers of the time, of which the names of Shah Tahmasp and Shah Abbas the Great stand out, were patrons of all the arts, but the carpets produced in this period have never been equalled anywhere. The leading artists of the day were commissioned to design these masterpieces, and the materials used were the finest obtainable. It is still not known where they were actually made; in fact it could be in any of the various cities where the court moved to during the many wars which were being waged during these troubled times.

The cities of Tabriz, Isfahan, Kazvin and Kashan are variously named as their birthplace, but it is more than likely that the carpet manufactory, together with its ancillary departments was carried around with the court as it moved. The few surviving carpets from this period are to be seen in those museums featuring Oriental textile art, but there must have been vast quantities made at the time. After the death of Shah Abbas the Great, the art gradually ceased to be important, and it reached its lowest point with the Afghan invasion of 1721. It did not recover until well into the nineteenth century. The revival was partly due to the interest of the then Shah, who was of the Qajar dynasty, and also to the re-awakening interest of the Western world in the craft. Tabriz became the centre of this revival at first, but it soon involved other towns and villages, and gradually an export business was built up with Tabriz as the main transit centre. Buyers came from all over Europe and America to Tabriz.

Western firms opened offices there and appointed buying agents, whilst local merchants shipped their wares to the markets of the West, and many went with their goods to become dealers in the principal cities of Europe and America. By the end of the nineteenth century a large business had been built up, not with the old traditional, long and narrow pieces, but with special designs and sizes to suit the houses of the new clientele. London became a particularly important transit market, as it still is, with vast warehouses filled with rugs and carpets from all over the Orient. Today's production however, quality-wise, apart from a few prestige pieces is but a shadow of that obtaining at the end of the nineteenth century. That is why the products of that period are so prized when they are found in good condition.

Turkey

It was the carpets from Turkey which first penetrated into Europe, through Venice, and the sixteenth and seventeenth centuries leave us in no doubt, through the efforts of the artists of the day in Europe, that there must have been a good trade in this commodity. All carpets entering England for instance were called 'Turkey' even though many of them were from other places. There was one notable exception to this. In 1518 Cardinal Wolsey asked the Venetian Ambassador for some 'Damascene' carpets. At that time wines were being imported into England from Candia by the Venetian merchants, and a duty was levied upon them which the

traders were anxious to have repealed. Were Cardinal Wolsey's request to be met, he promised to take the Ambassador before the Council, so that the envoy could argue for the repeal of the duties. Apparently the Cardinal received a few pieces during that year, but they do not seem to have satisfied his appetite, because he proceeded to demand a hundred 'Damascene' carpets in 1519 with the same promise contingent upon them.

Apart from this exception, all carpets, even English made pieces were called 'Turkish', although in the case of the latter, the preserved inventories read 'Turkey carpets of English making'. Carpets also entered Europe through another channel – Spain. Not directly however. They came via North Africa, due to the Moorish conquest of Spain. The Spanish people eventually established the manufacture of carpets in their own right, with Spanish inspired designs, and even a completely different system of knotting from that of the Orient. What is known as the 'Spanish' knot was evolved, and it remains to this day. Basically it is the Ghiordes or Turkish knot, but tied on one warp thread instead of on two. In each row of knots alternate warp threads are used. The Spanish carpet of the last two or three centuries therefore, whilst being Oriental in concept, is quite significantly different from its sister weave.

The earliest rugs of Turkey were of angular design, and many of them may have come from what we now know as the Caucasus. The port of Constantinople (Istanbul) was the clearing house for all the goods being exported to Europe, and there must have been many Caucasian and Persian pieces shipped, which on arrival were just designated as 'Turkish'. Even the famous carpet of the Worshipful Company of Girdlers in London was described in the minutes of the Company as a 'very faire long Turkey Carpitt' but we know it was made in India.

The Caucasus

The carpet producing parts of Russia are confined to two areas – the Caucasus and Turkestan. The former, sandwiched between the Black Sea and the Caspian, is the home of the pieces made with completely angular designs. No curves are to be found at all. The ornate and formal curvilinear designs developed in Persia in the sixteenth century did not penetrate into this wild, mountainous country. There is no organized manufacture as in Persia, and Turkey, it is purely a cottage and nomadic industry. The only carpets with any formality about them were the Armenian Dragon carpets of the fifteenth and sixteenth centuries. Usually attributed to Kuba, these highly stylized, so-called 'dragon' designed pieces were obviously made for use in houses, being in long and narrow sizes. Very few of these carpets are left, but most of the museums of Europe and America have at least one to show, if they feature Caucasians at all.

Other than this type, there do not appear to be many pieces from the Caucasus in existence dating from earlier than the second half of the eighteenth century, possibly because all their production was purely functional, there being no court production as in Persia, where the highest degree of artistic excellence was attained, for the sake of appearance.

The eighteenth and nineteenth century prayer rugs form the largest part of Caucasian production still in use. Prayer rugs to cover unclean ground are made and used by all people who profess the Moslem faith. They are colourful, extremely well made, and the materials used are first class, for the country is ideal for breeding the hardy sheep that give the tough springy wool which is necessary for floor coverings.

Western Turkestan – The Bokhara Weaves

Purely functional, with a variety of uses unknown in other parts of the Orient, the weavings of Western Turkestan owe nothing to the professional designer, although the resulting product is invariably a work of art.

Rugs, saddlebags, door hangings, gun covers, cushions, water bottle covers, tent bags and tent bands are just some of the ingenious articles made with hand knotted pile, all the trappings of a nomadic people, and all made for easy transportation during the frequent tribal movements.

In design, all Turkoman pieces have features distinguishing the tribe which made them, for there is no formal manufacture at all, the same designs being handed down through the generations. Historically, the products of this area must stem from a long ancestry, although the subject has never been fully explored. It was, of course, the original home of the Turks, and there is no reason to believe that the knotting art was not taken by them when they moved westwards, eventually to settle in Turkey. Consequently, the craft may have moved to the West rather than from it, as is popularly supposed. The ancient trade route from China passed through Turkestan, and although in neither case have we any direct evidence of early participation in the craft, the eminence of China in most other fields of art makes one think that the art of carpet knotting must have been mastered many centuries ago in that vast country.

Turkestan did not have any real communication with the Western world until after the Russian conquest late in the nineteenth century, and even then the flow of rugs out of the country was not considerable until well into the twentieth century. The nature of these goods, made by a primitive people, for use rather than ornament, and subject to abnormal wear by the very nature of their way of life, makes it impossible to put a date earlier than the beginning of the nineteenth century on any piece. The city of Bokhara is the market for goods being sold, and this name is used throughout the world to describe the products of this remote country. Actually, the tribal name should be used for accuracy, but there are many pitfalls in identification, for even though the tribes have their own motifs, many of these have been copied by other tribes, sometimes through marriage, or have become stylized, and are somewhat difficult to place. The main characteristic of the Turkoman weave is the brown to red ground colour, which is peculiar to this part of the world. It is very appropriate to this wild, cold and inhospitable country. Also usually featured is the motif, in one form or another, popularly known as the 'elephant's foot' design.

Eastern Turkestan – The Samarkand Weaves

Not very far to the east of Bokhara lies the ancient city of Samarkand. Not a carpet-making centre itself, Samarkand is a collecting centre for the products of the area very much to the east, and into Chinese Turkestan. Collectively known as 'Samarkand', these colourful pieces with both Chinese and Persian influence in them are really made in the vicinity of three important towns – Kashgar, Yarkand and Khotan.

As with Western Turkestan one cannot delve too deeply into the antiquity of these pieces, as there is no direct evidence to work on, but there is no doubt that rugs have been made in this part of the world for a very long time, even though there are no specific examples to show for it. Also, it is possible that instead of coming to the West, the products of this strange country went eastwards to grace the floors and walls of rich Chinese households. It was not until the nineteenth century that what we now regard as Samarkand rugs arrived in Europe. They must have been looked at with disdain, because they were coarse in comparison with the Persian weaves, and they lacked the finesse of the Persian designs. What they lacked in these respects however, were offset by their brilliant colours and complete contrast in configuration.

Commercially they were not a success, and very few people took the trouble to collect them, until the advent of the chemical washing process, when the interior decorators started to use them in their schemes, after the lovely bright colours had been removed, leaving them a wishy-washy shadow of their former beauty. Not only did the wash remove the colours, it also removed the firmness of the piece, and it handled like limp cloth.

Some pieces escaped this punishment, of course, and those now remain with us to illustrate the art of a primitive people, far removed from the civilized world as we know it, living in one of the most inaccessible parts of the world, and surrounded by some of the highest mountains in Asia.

Egypt – India – Kashmir – China

A craft which, so far as is known, spans a period of nearly 2,500 years, and which is still practised over a large part of the earth's surface, naturally has its areas where development was more pronounced than others; where the evolution of the people led them to greater heights in a particular field of enterprise, and where it was possible, in the age of Western exploration and exploitation, to study, at least superficially, the intricacies and history of the craft. Such is the case of the Oriental rug, and the previous sections have

discussed the areas best known and most open to Western study. The remaining areas, well known by name, have not made any significant contribution to the art of knotted textiles, but they have left a legacy of design technique which shows that copying is a two way traffic, and national considerations can over-ride the conquerors' whims, or the imported weavers' ideas. The prime example of national inspiration is Egypt. This country has a long record of textile production stretching back well into the pre-Christian era, but the earliest remains of what could conceivably be classified as knotted fabrics are some fragments of undoubtedly heavy cloth with a form of pile. These date from the fourth century AD. Opinion varies as to whether this fabric was made in the manner of Oriental rugs, or whether it was just a looped cloth rather in the nature of a Turkish towel. Some of the loops are cut, but whether this was done deliberately or through wear is not known.

The first examples of actual carpet knotting however, date from the Mameluke period, and these were made in Cairo. Although they were made with the Senneh or Persian knot, they certainly did not emulate any previously known designs. The nearest approach to these unique pieces would be the Caucasian, but even here the only resemblance was that both were angular in design rather than curvilinear.

The essence of these carpets was a rather indistinct design, usually not conventionally bordered, in three or four colours – red, green, blue, and yellow – giving the appearance of a mosaic rather than a textile fabric. This type of design persisted after the Ottoman conquest of 1517, but gradually the Turkish influence took over, and, no doubt due to the requirements of the Turkish court, the designs became more akin to those of Persia, with rounded forms, medallions, corner pieces and properly constructed borders. These designs, however, could never match the beautiful proportions and exquisite designing of the Persian examples.

For reasons not fully explained, the Cairo carpets have often been designated as 'Damascus'. Perhaps this stems from the demands of Cardinal Wolsey in 1518, who wanted 'Damascene' carpets, and possibly his demand was in perpetuation of the idea that these carpets bore some resemblance to the even then popular fabric known as damask.

There was no gentle decline in Egyptian carpets. There appears to have been an abrupt end to the weaving in the seventeenth century. This could be because the weavers were shipped off to work for their Turkish masters in Constantinople, leaving no more use for the looms of Cairo.

In discussing India it is necessary to include the whole of the sub-continent, including what is now known as Pakistan, and, of course, Kashmir. There is no evidence of carpet manufacture before the Moguls, although they were imported from Persia – particularly Kirman. However, the Emperor Akbar, with the help of Shah Abbas the Great of Persia, acquired Persian weavers, and started a manufactory in India. At first, as can be expected, the Persian designs were copied, and there is a class of carpet from the sixteenth and seventeenth centuries known as Indo-Isfahan, or Indo-Persian. Obviously, these were direct copies of Persian originals, or carpets made from designs prepared by Persian artists. India had, however,

some very good schools of design, practising all the arts, and gradually a change took place in carpet design, until a typical Indian design was developed. The centres of weaving were Agra and Lahore. There are not many early pieces left, and most of these cannot be identified with any particular centre of manufacture. The famous Girdlers carpet, however, still in the possession of the Worshipful Company of Girdlers in the City of London, has been well documented and it is recorded as having been made in Lahore.

Kashmir has for centuries been famous for textiles of one kind or another. There are no carpets of antiquity that can be attributed to this area, but a few very fine rugs were made about fifty years ago which for sheer fineness of weave have never been surpassed. The knotting—wool pile on silk warps—is in the order of 2,500/2,600 knots to the square inch. They appear to be scaled down replicas of the classical Persian originals. Whether they were samples, actual carpets for doll's houses, or just extravagant purchases made to order from princely families has never been confirmed. Useless as they are from a practical point of view, they are, however, of such technical importance that they should be preserved for posterity.

Rugs and carpets have probably been made in China for many centuries and records tell us that carpets were being used in 1122 BC, but not a vestige remains to offer any proof. It was the nineteenth century travellers who first brought back any information about the textile products of this vast country, and since that time a considerable industry has grown up to supply the needs of the Western markets. Of the antique pieces still in existence, most of them emanate from Pekin, but they are not as colourful as those pieces attributed to Ningsia and Sinkiang, which are more akin to the products of Eastern Turkestan than to China proper.

Classical Carpets

1 Ardebil Carpet (detail)

Found in a Mosque in Ardebil, north west Persia, this carpet is one of the finest examples extant of the work carried out during the Sefavi dynasty, the Golden Age of Persian production. The size is 34ft. 6in. × 17ft. 6in. and it is constructed with wool pile on silk foundation, the knotting being Senneh or Persian.

Apart from its beautifully balanced proportions and superb colours the most important feature is the cartouche at one end of the carpet. This reads: '*I have no refuge in the World other than thy threshold. There is no protection for my head other than this door. The work of the slave of the threshold Maksoud of Kashan in the year 946*'
This year in the Moslem Calendar corresponds with 1539/40 AD.

2 The Pazyryk Rug

What has now become known as the first ever hand knotted rug was discovered by the Russian archaeologist S. I. Rudenko during an expedition in 1947–9 to the Pazyryk valley of southern Siberia, a few miles from the Outer Mongolian border, in the region called Gorny Ältai. It was found in a burial mound, together with tapestries, felt wall hangings, chariots and leather work, all preserved by natural refrigeration – perennial ice. The rug is 6ft. 6in. × 6ft. oin. in size, of fairly fine knotting and is woven with the Ghiordes or Turkish knot. The design is Persian, and many of the motifs can be found in the Persian art of the time, and earlier. A general study of the articles found shows that the contents of the tomb date from the fifth century BC. In addition, the Pazyryk rug has been subjected to a radio-active carbon test with a result within a hundred years of this date.

2

3

4

5

3 Hunting Carpet (detail)
This is a smaller carpet than the Ardebil, being 18ft. 9in. × 12ft. 0in., but it is signed and dated, and is earlier than the masterpiece in the Victoria and Albert Museum.

There is some controversy as to the correct date owing to the fact that the figures are badly worked into the carpet, but a close study of the cartouche, which is in the centre of the piece, reveals that the most plausible date is 929 AH corresponding to 1523 AD and not 949 AH as some authorities suppose.

4 The Chelsea Carpet (detail)
So called because it was acquired by the Victoria & Albert Museum, London, around the beginning of the twentieth century from a dealer in Kings Road, Chelsea, this piece is another of the masterpieces of the world.

The size is 18ft. 0in. × 10ft. 0in. and like most of the other examples of the Sefavi period it is woven on a silk foundation with wool pile. It is not dated but it stems from the same period as the Ardebil carpet, although some authorities believe it is older, and the knotting is much finer.

5 Silk Hunting Carpet (detail)
The hunting designs in one form or another have been a favourite subject in Persian carpets for many centuries, and they are still popular even today. Hunting of course was always a royal pastime, and it was natural therefore that when the court painters were called upon to design carpets they should include this form of sport in their work.

This piece must rank amongst the finest of the world's carpets. Not only are the foundations of silk, but the pile also. Additionally, parts of the figures are brocaded in silver gilt. The weaving is very fine, as one would expect with silk, and it is far closer in weave than any of the other Sefavi carpets.

The size is 22ft. 9in. × 10ft. 7in.

6 7

6 Animal and Floral Carpet
Another popular subject for Persian
carpets is that of animals in combat.
Here is one of the finest to have come
down to us from the Sefavi period.
In the field flowers, large and small,
appear to blend in naturally with
animals, some fighting, some pursuing
their prey, dragons and birds, the
combination making what must be one
of the most superbly designed carpets
of all time. The inner guard border
consists of cartouches containing
inscriptions praising the carpet and
blessing the Shah.
As with all the classic carpets of this
period the warps and wefts are of silk,
whilst the knotted pile is wool.
Size 24ft. 11in. × 10ft 8in.

8

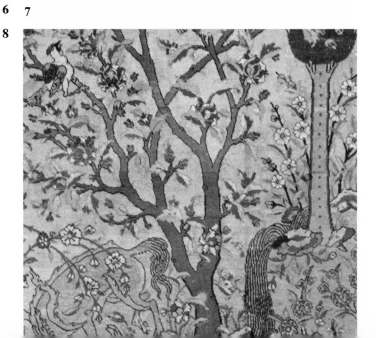

7 Animal and Floral Carpet with Medallion

Although much smaller than the Animal and Floral carpet in the Austrian Museum for Applied Art, the size being 16ft. 7in. × 7ft 11in., this is another fine example of Sefavi weaving in true tradition, with silk foundation and wool pile. In addition, it is embellished with gold and silver brocading. The inscription round the inner border praises the work of the artist who designed the piece, and in the poetic language of the time describes the features of the carpet.

8 Animal and Tree Carpet with Medallion (detail)

Here is a detail of one of the most popular designs to have come down to us from the Sefavi period. Half the carpet is in the Musée des Arts Décoratifs, Paris, the other half being in one of the state museums in Cracow (Krakow) Poland, having lain previously in the cathedral there. The Polish example was restored in 1968. The first mention of the half carpet in the French collection was in the early years of this century. It would appear therefore that the division was made sometime prior to this, although it is not known when, or why it was done. This design has been copied innumerable times, in many different fabrics, and even today it features in one British carpet manufacturer's range.

The size of the Paris fragment (shown here) is 13ft. 5in. × 11ft. 6in. whilst the restored Polish example measures 13ft. 0in. × 11ft. 10in.

9 The Ambassadors (detail) by Hans Holbein (1497–1543) painted in 1533.

Fifteen years before this picture was painted, Cardinal Wolsey was demanding 'Damascene' carpets from the Venetian Ambassador in London, and judging by the number of paintings by Italian and Dutch artists in this and the previous century showing carpets in European settings, many indeed must have been imported into Europe. Depending on their designs, some pieces are even today designated as 'Holbein' or 'Lotto' rugs, after the artists who used them.

Of course, not a vestige of any of the original rugs remains as far as is known, but without this pictorial evidence our knowledge of rugs and carpets of these early days would be scanty indeed.

9

Persia

10

10 Isfahan Carpet (detail)
There is a group of carpets, dating from the late sixteenth or early seventeenth centuries known as 'Vase' carpets, and examples can be seen, mainly in museums. They are attributed to Isfahan. In 1590 Shah Abbas the Great (of the Sefavi dynasty) moved his capital to this beautiful city, where it remained until the middle of the eighteenth century. With the court, it is natural to assume that the carpet manufactory also went, and it is possible that many of the classic Sefavi carpets were woven there.
The example illustrated is typical of the type.
Size 16ft. 0in. × 7ft. 8in.

11

11 Tabriz Carpet (detail)
The gateway to Persia from north and
west, Tabriz, has always been of
extreme importance, even to the
various conquerors from the eleventh
century, when it was overrun by the
Seljuk Turks. They introduced the
Turkish language, a dialect of which is
spoken there today. It was a capital city
in the Middle Ages, and is still of
course the principal city in the
province of Azerbaijan. The Tabriz
carpets and rugs most prized today
are those of the nineteenth century
revival of Persian weaving, and the
illustration is typical of the fine and
durable work done at that time.
Size 13ft. 2in. × 9ft. 5in.

12 Polonaise Rug
This piece is a classical example of the
so-called Polonaise silk, silver and gold
thread rug, which all authorities are
now convinced was made in Persia,
and not Poland as was thought at first.
Dating from the Sefavi period, rugs
and carpets of this nature were given to
royal and other high ranking person-
ages as gifts, particularly to Poland,
Sweden and Russia. Some even have
the recipients' coats of arms on them.
In common with other Sefavi products,
there is no evidence as to exactly where
they were made, but the general
opinion is that they were manufactured
during the reign of Shah Abbas the
Great, possibly in Isfahan.
Size 8ft. 0in. × 4ft. 4in.

Lately in the Kevorkian Foundation
Collection. Sold at Sotheby's,
London, 5 December 1969, Lot 5.

12

17 Tabriz Silk Rug

In addition to the skill of the weaver, great credit is due to the art of the designer, and nowhere is this more apparent than in these examples from Tabriz. It was the designer who actually created the piece in the first place, laboriously painting designs on squared paper, one little square for each knot of the carpet. This became the pattern from which the weavers worked.
Size 5ft. 1in. × 4ft. 2in.

18 Tabriz Rug

This rug again demonstrates the end product of the combined efforts of designer, colourist, spinner, weaver and finisher, for after weaving, all rugs and carpets must be cropped and washed in local waters.
Size 6ft. 0in. × 4ft. 8in.

19 Tabriz Silk Prayer Rug

Here is an interesting example of Tabriz weaving from the late nineteenth century. An unusual feature is the little row of arches above the *mihrab*.
Size 5ft. 0in. × 4ft. 0in.

20 Heriz Carpet (detail)

From the small town of Heriz, which lies about fifty miles east of Tabriz, together with its near neighbour Ghorovan, come some of the most easily recognizable of Persian carpets. Chiefly in medallion design on a brick-red ground colour, the curvilinear designs so typical of Persia have no place in the Heriz product. The designs are completely angular, a feature more in keeping with the Caucasus not far away to the north. There is no record of early antiquity in these products, but some very good pieces were made about a hundred years ago. These coarsely woven, colourful but tough carpets made the perfect setting for the oak dining rooms of the West, and even today some good pieces are made.

21 Heriz Carpet (detail)

Here is an example of modern work from Heriz. As will be noticed, the style does not change, and today it is one of the few types of Persian carpet which is kept up to a reasonable standard, that is, in the better qualities. Size 15ft. 1in. × 11ft. 7in.

22 Heriz Silk Rug

The silk rugs and carpets of Heriz bear some resemblance in design to those of Tabriz but they lack the sophistication of the latter, which is not surprising in view of the difference in the sizes of these two places. Tabriz could attract the best artists by virtue of its importance as a capital city.

In characteristic Heriz colouring, this finely woven, silk pile rug is a good example of late nineteenth century work from this small town. The change of colouring at the top end of the field is unusual, but it was done deliberately, presumably in order to establish the direction of the piece, which has a one way design. Size 6ft. 6in. × 4ft. 5in.

22

23

24

23 Heriz Silk Prayer Rug
This charming prayer rug, not unlike
a Tabriz in appearance, has an added
attraction in the inscription at the
foot of the piece.
Size 6ft 2in. × 3ft. 10in.

24 Heriz Silk (details)
Here are two illustrations in close-up
showing details of the intricate
patterns used in the products of Heriz.
Top from the field of a silk rug
Size 5ft. 10in. × 4ft. 11in.
Right detail of the field of a type of
design which has been popular in
Persia from time immemorial. This is
the 'garden design', where the field is
divided into 'plots' with various
flowers and trees in the sections. It all
creates a glorious illusion of a garden,
to be used in desert areas where there
is a lack of colour, for above all else,
the Persians love all things that grow,
and they are sadly missed in some of
the bleak parts of their country.
Size 12ft. 8in. × 8ft. 4in.

25 Senneh Rug
The official name of the home of the Senneh rug is Sanandaj. It is situated in the heart of Persian Kurdistan, not far from the Iraq border. The name of Senneh is well known in the rug world, for this is the name given to the Persian knot, as distinct from the Ghiordes or Turkish knot. This is in spite of the fact that most Senneh rugs are constructed with the Turkish knot, as are all Kurdish weaves. Senneh rugs are very supple, and are extremely finely woven. Also they are cropped very short, giving an appearance completely alien to the other Kurdish weaves, which are of very robust construction. It is indeed strange that this delicate type of rug should be confined to one small town in the vast area known as Kurdistan. The illustration shows one of the best known designs from Senneh. Size 6ft. 5in. × 4ft. 6in.

26 Senneh Rug
Another popular design from Senneh, this time in a pine cone or leaf pattern. This particular motif is used extensively in Persia, in one form or another, particularly in Senneh, Kirman and Khorassan.
Size 6ft. 6in. × 4ft. 4in.

27 Saruk Rug

Hamadan, the Ecbatana of ancient times, is the market for the products of some hundreds of villages in the surrounding neighbourhood, and many European buying houses have offices and agencies there. Many of the rugs and carpets handled are dubbed by the traders as 'Hamadan', particularly the long runners of which a large number are made in this area. Some types of rug however have separate identities, and one such type is the Saruk, made in a small place of that name, but marketed in Hamadan.

The Saruk rug of the nineteenth century is a very finely woven and short cropped piece, and the illustration shows the resulting clarity of design, which can only be obtained with fine yarns, fine knotting and short cropping. The Saruk of today bears little resemblance to the above description, but it is very popular in America, which calls for a very heavy, high piled, luxurious-looking piece, and buys it in quantity.
Size 6ft. 5in. × 4ft. 5in.

28 Saruk Rug

The wealth of detail in the design of this fine late nineteenth century piece can be clearly seen, due to the techniques of the Saruk weavers at that time. Such rugs are getting more scarce as time goes by.
Size 6ft. 11in. × 4ft. 6in.

34 Kashan Silk Carpet (detail)
As with wool, so did Kashan make some very fine silk carpets and rugs during the nineteenth century revival of the craft.

This illustration shows part of the field design of a medium-sized carpet. The silk and wool products of today from Kashan are however poor in comparison. The materials are inferior to those used in the past, and the designs and colours are monotonous. Occasionally a good piece is made, but it is very expensive when it arrives on the market.
Size 12ft. 2in. × 8ft. 1in.

35 Kashan Rug
A further example of the designer's and weaver's skill from the early days of this century–a 'vase' design.
Size 5ft. 3in. × 3ft. 8in.

32 Kashan Rug
A good example of the art of the Kashan school of designing. A 'vase' rug, superbly drawn, and finely executed.
Size 6ft. 6in. × 4ft. 6in.

33 Kashan Rug
Rather older than the rug in the preceding illustration, the merits of this rug rely on the rich colours and the magnificent wool with which it was made. It is now in the peak of condition and with care will remain so for a long time to come.
Size 6ft. 1in. × 4ft. 4in.

34

36

38

37

36 Kashan Silk Rug
A tree design in the field, and the main border completely covered with inscriptions. Such a combination of designing skill and calligraphy is not unique, but this particular example shows just how cleverly the two skills can be married when in the hands of the Kashani school.
Size 5ft. 1in. × 3ft. 5in.

37 Part Silk Qum Rug
About half-way between Kashan and the capital of Persia – Teheran – lies the town of Qum. It is second only to Meshed as a place of pilgrimage, for here is buried the sister of the eighth Imam of the Moslem faith, and also some Sefavi and Qajar kings.
Weaving only started here between the two world wars, as a cottage industry, and some new designs were created by an excellent school of artists. The rugs and carpets were executed in both wool, and wool with some silk in the pile. The illustration shows a piece worked in the latter medium.
Size 7ft. 0in. × 4ft. 10in.

38 Shiraz Rug (Quashqai)

The most southerly of the places traditionally associated with carpets, Shiraz is situated in the south-west of the country. It is the capital city of the province of Fars, where most of the so-called Shiraz rugs are made by the tribes of the area, mainly the Quash-qais. Another tribe, the Afsharis live in the area between Shiraz and Kir-man, and dispose of their products in both markets.

Shiraz conjures up romantic thoughts of rose gardens and poets, and it is indeed a beautiful city, but for our purpose it is only the market place for the surrounding area.

Size 8ft. 6in. × 5ft. 0in.

39 Bakhtiari Carpet

The Bakhtiari tribe is one of the largest in Persia, and whilst the majority of its members still live nomadically, a number of them settled in villages something over a century ago in an area west of Isfahan, and it is this section which makes the colourful products known in the markets as Bakhtiari. These are rather coarsely woven, and their rather formal design-ing belies their nomadic origin.

Size 18ft. 9in. × 11ft. 3in.

39

40

40 Laver Kirman Rug
Made in a small place not far from
Kirman, this rug has the pine cone or
leaf design reminiscent of the earlier
trade in shawls.
Size 6ft. 5in. × 4ft. 2in.

41 Kirman Carpet (detail)
This old city, situated on the southern
edge of the desert, which covers a large
portion of central Persia, bears a time-
honoured name in textiles. Rugs and
carpets were being made in the Sefavi
period, even to the extent of exporting
them to India.
With the revival of the craft in the
nineteenth century Kirman became
well known, not for carpets, but in the
making of shawls. These were made in
the pine cone or leaf design, similar to
Kashmir shawls, and also of course to
the Paisley shawls of Scotland. These
latter killed the Eastern market, when
power driven looms and the ability to
print designs became practicable.
When carpet weaving became important again, in the second half of the
nineteenth century the Kirman
products found a market in the West.
Always wonderful designers of floral
motifs, the pieces were closely woven,
of good wool and excellent definition
of design. The present-day, chemically
washed, so called 'American Kirmans'
bear no relationship to the earlier
masterpieces apart from the fact that
they still produce wonderful designs.
Size 15ft. 5in. × 10ft. 2in.

42 Kirman Carpet (detail)
A typical example of Kirmani design-
ing of a centre medallion carpet.
Size 13ft. 2in. × 9ft. 9in.

43 Quashqai Kelleye
Although small for a Kelleye, this
piece has the right proportions. Made
by the Quashqai tribe in the vicinity of
Shiraz, this colourful example shows
just how intricate a pattern can be
executed by a nomadic people.
Size 10ft. 3in. × 5ft. 3in.

41

42

43

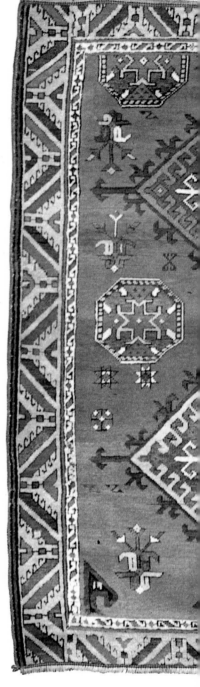

55

56

55 Ghiordes Prayer Rug
This small town gave its name to one of
the two basic knots used to weave
Oriental carpets wherever they are
made. There are various types of
Ghiordes rug, but this illustration is of
what is probably the finest weave. It is
called a Basra Ghiordes and dates from
the seventeenth century. The decoration hanging in the *mihrab* represents a
mosque lamp, which helps to give the
user a feeling of being in a holy place no
matter where the rug is laid.
Size 5ft. 6in. × 4ft. 3in.

56 Konia Rug
There is a distinct Caucasian flavour
to the design of this rug, which suggests
that it was made by weavers imported
from the Caucasus, or designed by
someone who had been there.
Size 5ft. 5in. × 3ft. 8in.

46

57 Ghiordes Prayer Rug
Another version of the type known as Basra Ghiordes.
Size 5ft. 9in. × 4ft. 4in.

58 Konia Prayer Rug
Until the discovery of the Pazyryk rug, nearly a quarter of a century ago, the oldest fragments known were those exhibited in the Museum of Islamic Art, Istanbul, and these were found in the mosque of Ala-ad-din, in Konia. They are reputed to date from the thirteenth century, and naturally are supposed to have been made in Konia,

or at least, in the vicinity. Once the capital city of Seljuki Turks, this ancient city was originally known as Iconium.

The illustration is of a prayer rug from the early eighteenth century. When spread on the ground for the purpose of prayer the *mihrab* is pointed in the direction of Mecca, the Holy City. Inside all mosques there is a *mihrab* built into one of the walls indicating the right direction.
Size 4ft. 1in. × 3ft 3in.

59 Ghiordes Prayer Rug
Here is a later example of the Ghiordes
weave. The *mihrab* has become rounded, and in the panel above it there are
two inscriptions.
Size 4ft. 4in. × 3ft. 4in.

60 Ghiordes Rug
A further kind of Ghiordes rug is
exemplified in these colourful small
pieces, which are always of similar
design to the illustration. They are the
Kiz-Ghiordes rugs of the late eighteenth century. The prefix Kiz means
'maiden' and these rugs were reputedly
woven by young girls as part of their
dowry, or to show their prowess as
weavers to their prospective bride-
grooms.
Size 4ft. 3in. × 3ft. 9in.

61 Ghiordes Rug
An unusual example from the looms of
Ghiordes, this rug was made in the
middle of the nineteenth century.
Around this time there was a vogue in
Turkey for furniture and accessories in
the French style, particularly at court,
and amongst high ranking officials and
diplomats. At this time also, Turkey
imported carpets for court use, and
both the Axminster hand knotted factory, and the Wilton factory in England
supplied hand knotted carpets for the
Sultan.
Size 5ft. 10in. × 3ft. 7in.

62   63

62 Koula Rug

Not very far from Ghiordes lies the small town of Koula. It is reputed to have been a weaving centre in the seventeenth and eighteenth centuries. What mainly remains today from this period is a series of prayer rugs, somewhat coarser and less colourful than their contemporaries from Ghiordes. The rug illustrated is of a type known as Mezarlik Koula or 'tomb rug', supposedly used to cover the tombs of high ranking people. The main feature of the Mezarlik rug is the two rows of designs bearing a resemblance to cypress trees, within the centre field.
Size 6ft. 9in. × 4ft. 2in.

63 Ladik Prayer Rug

There are many places in the Middle East named Laodicea (the modern port in Syria, once known by that name is now called Al Ladhiqiyah), but the Ladik rug is popularly supposed to have been made in or near to the Laodicea (now a ruin) adjacent to the town of Denizli in south west Anatolia. It is by no means certain, but at least this particular Laodicea is in a traditional rug-making area, and it is feasible to suggest that the word Ladik is a corruption of this name. Ladik rugs are rare, always in prayer design, and they feature long-stemmed tulips, normally at the top of the piece, dividing three *mihrabs*. The rug illustrated, from the late eighteenth century, appears to be a 'double ended' prayer rug. The picture has been printed with the single *mihrab* uppermost, but it could equally well have been depicted the other way round.
Size 6ft. 7in. × 3ft. 8in.

64 Ladik Prayer Rug

A fine example of the Ladik prayer rug, this time with a date. It is 1216 AH which corresponds to the year 1801 AD.
Size 6ft. 7in. × 4ft. 3in.

65 Sivas Silk Rug
There is no historical significance in
the rugs from Sivas. The manufactory
flourished in the nineteenth century,
when very good copies of Persian and
European pieces were made. They
command high prices in today's
markets, due to the excellence of the
materials used and the fine weaving.
Almost always made in finely spun
wool, there can occasionally be found
rugs and carpets of silk, as the illustration shows.
Size 6ft. 5in. × 4ft. 6in.

65

66 Melas Prayer Rug
A few miles inland from the Aegean
Sea lies the small town of Melas. It has
no early history of rug making, but
nevertheless, some very colourful
specimens have emanated from the
cottage industry worked there. The
piece illustrated is not of a typical
design, being rather one of the rarer
examples.
Size 5ft. 9in. × 3ft. 10in.

67 Melas Rug
Again not typical, this is one of the few
examples of a Melas rug of non-prayer
design. Rather coarsely woven in comparison with the Ghiordes rugs, yet
these pieces portray a blend of colours
and a sophistication of design that
would do justice to the finest artists and
colourists from the large cities.
Size 5ft. 6in. × 3ft. 4in.

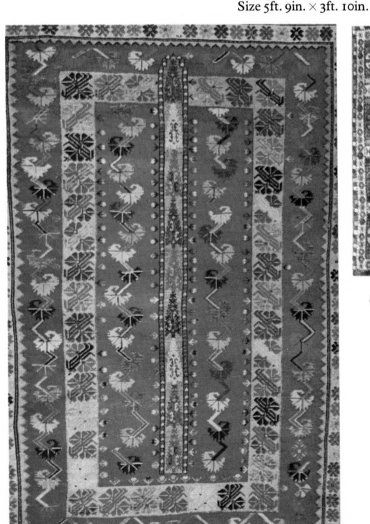

66

67

68 Hereke Silk Rug
This small town was the scene of a
royal manufactory during the nineteenth century, when some very finely
woven pieces were made, from wool as
well as silk. Some had a French flavour,
whilst others were magnificent copies
of traditional Persian designs. Many
were given as gifts by the Sultan to
high ranking visitors, and most of the
crowned heads of Europe possessed at
least one rug.
Size 6ft. 0in. × 4ft. 2in.

Turkey in Europe

70 Late Sixteenth Century Prayer Rug

This distinctive class of rug has been described over the years as of Persian court manufacture, having supposedly been made in any one of the towns where the court settled during these war torn years. However, it has recently been revealed that a collection of similar pieces is in the possession of the Top-Kapi Serai in Istanbul, and it is now thought that these exquisite rugs were made there for the use of members of the court. The weavers were most likely to be Persians.
Size 5ft. 5in. × 3ft. 11in.

71 Feshane Carpet (detail)

The carpet of which this illustration is a detail, was made at a royal manufactory situated in the environs of Istanbul, in the middle of the nineteenth century, and it copies faithfully the style of the French Savonnerie carpets, then in vogue in Turkey.
Size 14ft. 2in. × 10ft. 2in.

70

69 Hereke Silk Prayer Rug

Beautifully executed, this extremely fine silk rug has all the beauty one associates with royal manufacture. Obviously designed by a first class artist, who must also have been an expert colourist, and made with top grade materials, it is a perfect example of nineteenth century Hereke workmanship.
Size 5ft. 9in. × 4ft. 1in.

71

The Caucasus

72 Daghestan Prayer Rug

Sandwiched between the Black Sea and the Caspian, this area, now Russian, is the home of the pieces made with completely angular designs. There is no organized manufacture as in Persia and Turkey, it is purely a cottage and nomadic industry. Apart from the so-called 'Armenian Dragon' carpets of the fifteenth and sixteenth centuries, there do not appear to be many Caucasian pieces in existence earlier than the second half of the eighteenth century, possibly because all their production was purely functional.

Many nineteenth century prayer rugs are still in use. They are colourful, extremely well made and the materials used are first class, as the country is ideal for breeding the hardy sheep that give the tough springy wool necessary for floor coverings. This prayer rug is from the area in the north east of the country known as Daghestan.
Size 4ft. 7in. × 3ft. 10in.

73 Derbend Rug

Of coarser weave than the rugs of neighbouring Daghestan, the Derbend rugs from the city of that name on the Caspian Sea are also more dull in appearance as the example shows.
Size 4ft. 8in. × 3ft. 2in.

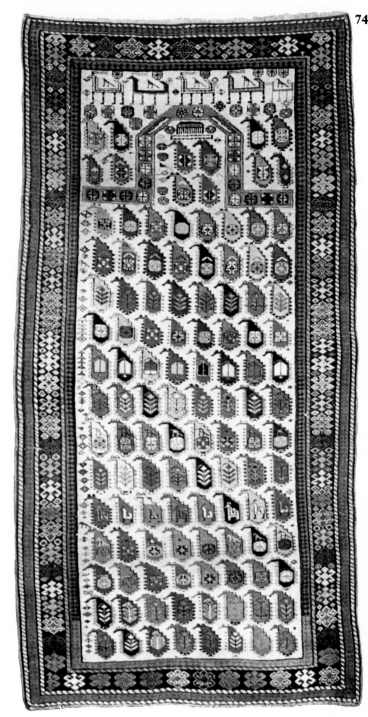

74

74 Daghestan Prayer Rug
The beauty of this rug lies in the artistic balance of colours which its creator has been able to achieve, whilst at the same time filling the piece with the most exquisite ornament. It is interesting to note that there are 116 pine cone or *boteh* motifs in the rug, each one being different to its fellows, and in addition, the rug manages to include *mihrab*, comb, animals and birds, and many small jewel-like objects in the field and around the *mihrab*. The rug is very finely woven, and closely cropped to give wonderful clarity of design.
Size 6ft. 0in. × 3ft. 0in.

75

75 Daghestan Prayer Rug
Most Daghestan rugs are of the prayer variety, with much ornament in the field. They are tightly woven, of high quality wool. This example is typical of the area.
Size 5ft. 9in. × 3ft. 8in.

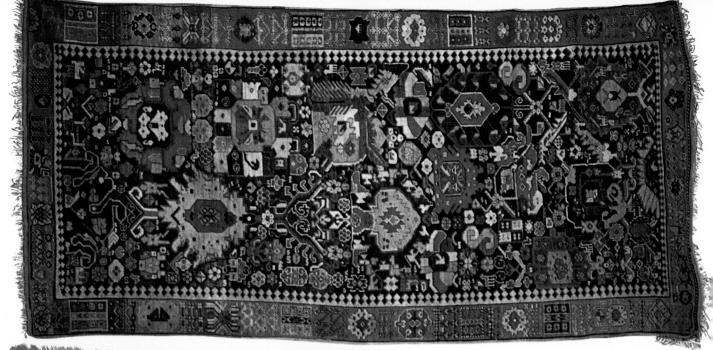

76 Kuba Carpet
To the south of Daghestan lies Kuba, which with the Shirvan district makes up the largest of the Caucasian weaving areas. Kuba is supposedly the place where the 'Armenian Dragon' carpets were made, but there is no direct evidence to support this view. The illustration shows an eighteenth century piece which was probably made for a good class household, for Kuba is a large trading centre.
Size 12ft. 6in. × 6ft. 2in.

77 Lesghi Prayer Rug
These rugs come from an area to the north of Daghestan, inhabited by a tribe known as the Lesghians. A fine example of the acute colour sense of these tribesmen is portrayed in this prayer rug, which, in spite of its primitive design, has a beauty not always matched by more sophisticated pieces.
Size 5ft. 5in. × 3ft. 1in.

78 Lesghi Rug
The products of the Lesghian tribesmen are very similar to those of Daghestan, but they tend to use a lot of bright yellow and green, which blend remarkably well.
Size 4ft. 11in. × 3ft. 11in.

79 Chichi Rug
Not very far from Kuba the village of Chichi produces some rather attractive and easily recognizable rugs. The chief characteristic of the Chichi rug is the main border treatment consisting of oblique bands alternating with stylized flower heads. Also the field is usually filled to capacity with stylized flower heads.
Size 4ft. 9in. × 3ft. 9in.

78

79

80

80 Chichi Prayer Rug
It is unusual to see a Chichi with prayer design, but here again, the main border is in keeping with all the rugs from this village.
Size 4ft. 10in. × 3ft. 6in.

81 Seichur Rug
These rugs come from a small place to the north of Kuba, and although this example is not typical of the make, it has the rose-red colouring in the main motifs with which the Seichur is associated.
Size 4ft. 5in. × 3ft. 3in.

82 Shirvan Prayer Rug
Finely woven, and with a short cropped pile, this nineteenth century Shirvan reveals the clarity of design which makes these pieces so attractive and sought after.
Size 4ft. 9in. × 3ft. 5in.

83 Shirvan Prayer Rug
A further example of nineteenth century Shirvan weaving.
Size 4ft. 5in. × 3ft. 5in.

81

82   83

84 Shirvan Prayer Rug
There are comparatively few old Shirvan prayer rugs still existing from what must have been quite a large production. This rug is typical of the area, with its angular designing, stylized motifs and the absence of the pillars which are a feature of the prayer rugs from Turkey.
Size 5ft. 8in. × 3ft. 6in.

85 Shirvan Rug
Occasionally, a piece from a given area can be identified as coming from a particular village, or at least that the design is associated with that village. Such a piece is this one illustrated here. The village is Perepedil to the north of Kuba and both the field and border designs of this example are often used here. For the purposes of trade, however, the name Shirvan is applied to such pieces.
Size 9ft. 1in. × 5ft. 1in.

86 Shirvan Rug and detail
The large peacock-like figures in the
field identify this piece as probably
coming from the town of Akstafa in the
west of the Shirvan area. Designs,
however, are copied over and over
again in various parts of the country,
and that is another reason for such
pieces to be designated Shirvan in the
bazaars and markets of the world.
Size 8ft. 6in. × 4ft. 7in.

86

87

88

87 Kazak Rug
The south west Caucasus, between
Tiflis, the capital of Georgia, and
Erevan, the capital of Armenia, is the
home of these well known rugs. Many
Oriental colourists use green, some-
times not very successfully. In this rug,

89

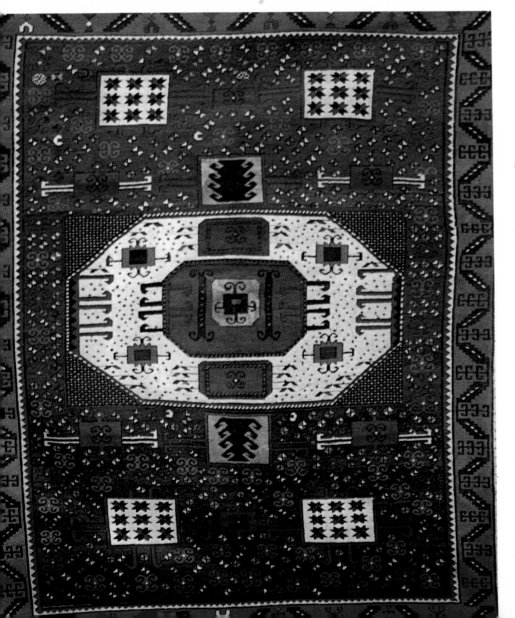

however, the dyer appears to have excelled himself. Remarkably so, in view of the wild region where this piece was made by nomads or at best, village dwellers, who not only produced the woven fabric but the excellent materials with which it is made.
Size 6ft. 6in. × 4ft. 6in.

88 Kazak Rug
Another typical piece from the Kazak area, showing once again how successfully the use of green can be employed.
Size 7ft. 7in. × 6ft. 6in.

89 Kazak Rug
This piece shows the boldness of the Kazak designing. Some authorities say that the cross denotes that it was made by Armenian weavers, who of course would be Christians, but this has not been authenticated.
Size 6ft. 4in. × 5ft. 1in.

90

91

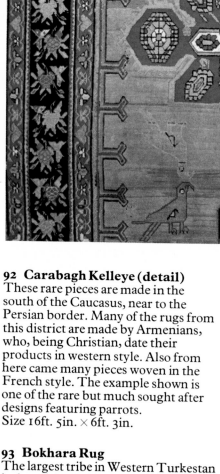

92

90 Baku (Hile) Rug
Marketed in the oil town of Baku on the coast of the Caspian Sea, these rugs are made in the nearby town of Hile. This particular type of rug is known as the 'Boteh Hile' identifying the *boteh* or pine cone motifs in the field.
Size 9ft. 2in. × 4ft. 4in.

91 Genje Runner
These pieces are made in the Kazak area, and are very similar in weave. The design illustrated is typical, with its diagonal stripes.
Size 8ft. 6in. × 3ft. 9in.

92 Carabagh Kelleye (detail)
These rare pieces are made in the south of the Caucasus, near to the Persian border. Many of the rugs from this district are made by Armenians, who, being Christian, date their products in western style. Also from here came many pieces woven in the French style. The example shown is one of the rare but much sought after designs featuring parrots.
Size 16ft. 5in. × 6ft. 3in.

93 Bokhara Rug
The largest tribe in Western Turkestan is that of the Tekkes, who inhabit the border country touching Persia, even spilling over into the latter, which is why some so-called Bokhara rugs are

brought to the west through the markets of Persia itself. The illustration is of a typical rug made by these people.
Size 7ft. 10in. × 4ft. 0in.

94 Yamout Bokhara Tent Bag
This is one of the most useful of the many domestic articles from western Turkestan – a tent bag, made by the Yamout tribe. Often these are of unusually fine work, and in addition to their value as a receptacle in the home, they are extremely decorative. The typical Turkoman colouring adds a touch of warmth to tent life. Yamout rugs are also found in Persia, as parts of this tribe also inhabit the north eastern part of this country.
Size 4ft. 4in. × 2ft. 6in.

Western Turkestan

93

94

95 Hatchli Bokhara Prayer Rug

The name Hatchli is given to Turko-man rugs bearing the design of a cross in the field. Reputedly they are used as tent doorways, but some of them, as the illustration shows, have a rather unobtrusive *mihrab*, signifying that they are for prayer use.
Size 5ft. oin. × 3ft. 11in.

96 Bokhara Prayer Rug

A rather unusual rug of prayer design, but showing the unobtrusive form of the Bokhara *mihrab*, probably made by the Salor tribe. The products of the Turkomans have never received the attention they deserve by Western collectors. The reasons for this may be that the country itself is almost un-known; that there is no yardstick for denoting the age of the rugs, and, to the layman at least, there is a certain monotony of design and colour. Certainly the Bokhara design is most easily recognized by everyone, and it has been copied in all manner of fabrics throughout the world. The typical ground colour and the inoffensive small all-over motifs lend themselves to the warm and homely furnishing schemes in the West. They are easily assimilated into almost any period of decoration, and consequently should have an appeal which far outweighs the general knowledge of them.
Size 4ft. 3in. × 3ft. 5in.

97 Samarkand Rug

There can be no mistaking the Chinese influence in this beautiful piece of workmanship from Central Asia.
Size 8ft. 8in. × 4ft. 9in.

98 Samarkand Saph

A very fine example of a Saph or multiple prayer design from eastern Turkestan, and marketed in Samar-kand. The only other place where such pieces are found is Turkey. This piece is made of wool, but some examples are made in this style with silk pile. The compartments are, of course, much too small for the piece to be used in the conventional way. These runners are used as mosque decoration, and as floor coverings.
Size 13ft. 4in. × 3ft. 7in.

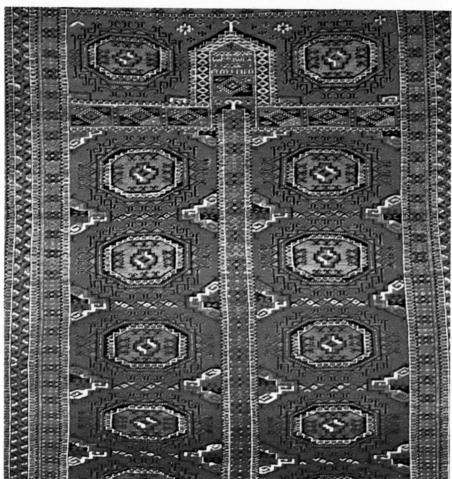

Eastern Turkestan

97

98

Egypt-India-Kashmir-China

99

100

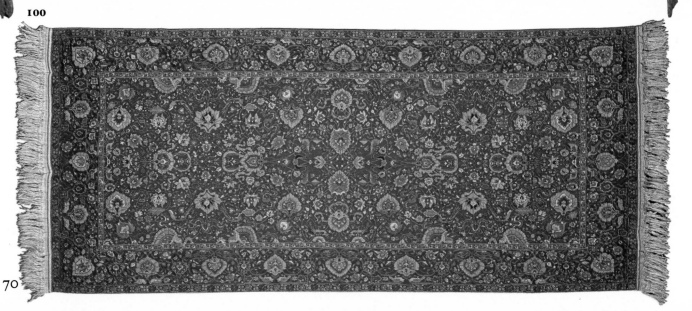

70

99 Chinese Silk Rug
This is an unusual example to show of
Chinese work; a more obvious one
would have been the typical Pekin
product of the nineteenth century,
before modern techniques and western
demands created the so-called 'super-
washed Chinese carpet'. However,
this piece gives a good idea of the kind
of intricate weaving in silk that the
Chinese were capable of doing in the
last century, and it suggests that they
were not newcomers to the scene at the
time.
Size 8ft. 3in. × 5ft. 4in.

100 A Carpet in Miniature
Woven in wool on a silk foundation,
with a small amount of silk in the pile,
this is one of the finest examples of
carpet knotting ever produced. There
are between fifty and fifty two knots
per inch each way, making about 2,600
knots to the square inch, a total of
almost three million individual knots
in the whole piece. It is a scaled-down
reproduction, knot for knot, of an
original sixteenth century Persian
carpet. It was made in Kashmir,
probably about the end of the nineteenth or the beginning of the twentieth
century.
Size 4ft. 3in. × 1ft. 10in.

**101 Mameluke Carpet from Cairo
(detail)**
A late fifteenth or early sixteenth century example from the looms of Cairo.
These and the later Turkish inspired
designs used after the Ottoman conquest are sometimes erroneously
described as 'Syrian' or 'Damascus'
carpets.
Size unrecorded.

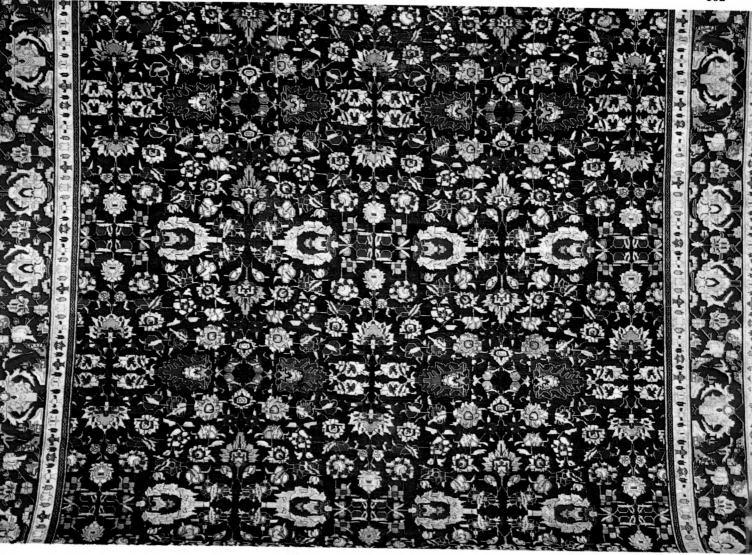

102 Agra Carpet (detail)
The Agra carpets of the nineteenth century, are, along with the Persian Bijar carpets, the heaviest of all the Oriental weaves. This example is typical of the work of this period. Size 14ft. 9in. × 11ft. 3in.

Acknowledgments

The Publisher wishes to thank the following for supplying photographs for the plates in this book:

Austrian Museum for Applied Art, Vienna : 5, 6 ; British Museum, London : 49 ; Collezione Pogliaghi, Milan : 101 ; Fratelli Fabbri Editori, Milan : 20 ; Hermitage Museum, Leningrad : 2 ; Musée des Arts Décoratifs, Paris : 8 ; Museo Poldi Pezzoli, Milan : 3, 7 ; National Gallery, London : 9 ; Perez (London) Ltd : 10, 12–19, 21–48, 50–100, 102 ; Sotheby's : 11 ; Victoria and Albert Museum : 1, 4.